Saloon Singer

Frank Sinatra in His Own Words
And in the Words of Those Who Knew Him

By Michael Turback
Author of *All the Gin Joints*

Saloon Singer

Frank Sinatra in His Own Words
And in the Words of Those Who Knew Him

Printed in the United States of America.

DEDICATION

*To the skinny kid from Hoboken
who had a dream.*

"Being a saloon singer, that's my racket."
— Frank Sinatra

In his heyday, it was said, "Every woman wants to have him; every man wants to be him." The "him" was Francis Albert Sinatra, a singer whose aching baritone set a standard for the romantic ballad that has never been equaled, and whose dynamic lifestyle and charismatic persona made his artistic contribution that much more compelling.

Raised in a rough Jersey neighborhood, the skinny kid needed every scrap of his trademark pugnacity to get by. As a teenager, he organized a quartet dubbed the "Hoboken Four," then plugged away as a singing waiter before joining the Harry James orchestra as male vocalist. Within six months, Tommy Dorsey came calling, and the collaboration resulted in a string of hit singles. By 1943, he parted ways with Dorsey and embarked on the solo career that made him a legend.

This fizzy cocktail of a book provides an unvarnished portrait of a scrappy underdog who occupies a unique place in the pantheon of American popular culture. You get a little history and a bit of sociology. But the fun comes from an abundant helping of irreverence in this excerpted study of a complicated and enigmatic figure. His contemporaries as well as subsequent observers have plenty to say about Sinatra – he's tough and tender, a lover and a fighter, a star and a loner – and his own brash words provide an affectionate, perceptive portrait of the man who is called the greatest entertainer of all time .

Michael Turback

"I'm going to be the best singer in the world, the best singer that ever was."

— Frank Sinatra

"To Sinatra, a microphone is as real as a girl waiting to be kissed."

— E. B. White, *The New Yorker*

"I am a thing of beauty."

— Frank Sinatra

"He's just beautiful. To me, he is a 'pigeon-blood' ruby and that's the greatest ruby there is!"

— Count Basie

"I first knew Frank in the Dorsey days and his singing has affected me ever since. He is an original, quite unique. His magic is a combination of many things but mainly, I guess, the texture of the voice itself and the charisma of the man."

— Harold Arlen

"He's a hell of a guy. He tries to live his own life. I like his style."

— Humphrey Bogart

"He is a remarkable personality – tough, vulnerable and somehow touching."

— Noel Coward

"I'm a performer. I'm better in the first take."

— Frank Sinatra

"He cannot read music, yet he has taken popular singing and made of it an art. He is the finest living singer of popular songs."

— Thomas Thompson

"At heart, I'm a saloon singer because there's a greater intimacy between performer and audience in a nightclub."

— Frank Sinatra

"My greatest teacher was not a vocal coach, not the work of other singers, but the way Tommy Dorsey breathed and phrased on the trombone. The thing that influenced me most was the way Tommy played his trombone. It was my idea to make my voice work in the same way as a trombone or violin – not sounding like them, but 'playing' the voice like those instrumentalists."

— Frank Sinatra

"There's no one like him. It's not only that his intuitions as to tempo, phrasing, and even configuration are amazingly right, but his taste is so impeccable. When he's moving, get the hell out of the way. When he's doing nothing, move in fast and establish something. After all, what arranger in his right mind would try to fight against Sinatra's voice?"

— Nelson Riddle

"Let's face it, Sinatra is a king. He's a very sharp operator, a keen record chief, and has a keen appreciation of what the public wants."

— Bing Crosby

"Regardless of his arranger or conductor or who was listed as producer, Sinatra was the arbiter of how the final take should sound."

— Francis Davis

"He is better than anybody else, or at least they think he is, and he has to live up to it.'"

— Nancy Sinatra

"Throughout my career, if I have done any-thing, I have paid attention to every note and every word I sing – if I respect the song. If I cannot project this to a listener, I fail."

— Frank Sinatra

"What is the point of singing wonderful lyrics if the audience can't understand what is being said or heard?"

— Frank Sinatra

"Whatever else has been said about me personally is unimportant. When I sing, I believe. I'm honest."

— Frank Sinatra

"I think his great ability is to make the listener feel and understand the lyric, to impart exactly what the composer had in mind, which is a vital thing. When Frank sings a torch song, if you have ever torched, you know what he's singing about.'"

— William B. Williams

"I always believed that the written word was first, always first. Not belittling the music behind me, it's really only a curtain. The word actually dictates to you in a song – it really tells you what it needs."

— Frank Sinatra

"He sings and lives in the lyric."

— Robert Merrill

"You begin to learn to use the lyrics of a song as a script, as a scene."

— Frank Sinatra

"He moved into a lyric like it was his house."

— Sammy Cahn

"The way he sang lyrics, everybody thought he was singing right to them."

— Nancy Reagan

"I don't know what other singers feel when they articulate lyrics, but being an 18-karat manic-depressive and having lived a life of violent emotional contradictions, I have an over acute capacity for sadness as well as elation."

— Frank Sinatra

"Frank is one of the three greatest influences vocally, in my life, along with Big Crosby and Fred Astaire. I feel that Frank has to be one of the two of three greatest delineators of a lyric and he understood very early on that the lyric was 98 per cent of what was important about a song."

— Mel Tormé

"When I get a new song, I look for continuity of melody that in itself will tell a musical story. It must go somewhere. I don't like it to ramble."

— Frank Sinatra

"I saw complete and utter involvement with the song he was singing – involvement that one might feel he was in the throes of composing both tune and lyric as he went along."

— Robin Douglas-Home

"The microphone is the singer's basic instrument. You have to learn to play it like it was a saxophone."

— Frank Sinatra

"I use all the color changes I can get into my voice. The microphone catches the softest tone – a whisper."

— Frank Sinatra

"When he was young, in the '40s, he was a violin. In the '50s, he was a viola. By the '60s, he was a cello and when he got to the '80s, he was a bass."

— Sammy Cahn

"I get an audience involved, personally involved in a song – because I'm involved myself. It's not something I do deliberately;
I can't help myself. If the song is a lament at
the loss of love, I get an ache in my gut, I feel
the loss myself and I cry out the loneliness,
the hurt and the pain that I feel."

— Frank Sinatra

"He achieved a musical conversation with his audience. He seemed to understand better than anyone the conundrum of love – how hard it is for two people to be at the same emotional place at the same time."

— David Halberstam

"There are times if I want to do something that has a lonely effect, we go back to the [solo] piano or an alto saxophone as part of the orchestration."

— Frank Sinatra

"When he sang about loneliness, it's because he had experienced the deepest sorrow and despair, and we are all aware of the happiness, the delight, he felt singing the other songs, be they ballads or up-tempo – because, if we are not looking at him, we can, literally, hear him smile."

— Nancy Sinatra

"People who understand music hear sounds that no one else makes when Sinatra sings."

— Walter Cronkite

"Frank brought out my best work. He's stimu-
lating to work with. You have to be right on
mettle all the time. The man somehow draws
everything out of you. He has the same effect
on the boys in the band – they know he means
business so they pull everything out."

— Nelson Riddle

"It is Billie Holiday who was, and still remains, the greatest single musical influence on me."

— Frank Sinatra

"Frank is a singer who comes along once in a lifetime, but why did he have to come in my lifetime?"

— Bing Crosby

"His audience was absolutely and without reservation his. He'd never allow their attention or focus to stray."

— Shirley MacLaine

"If Frank Sinatra is singing a sad song, he reminds you of every moment when you were ever sad. He puts you into that, if you lost your girl and he is singing about a lost love, you totally feel that loss through his voice, and on the other hand when he is singing a happy song, an up tempo song, that reminds you of the happiest times of your life."

— Anthony Quinn

"Critics don't bother me because if I do badly, I know I'm bad before they even write it. And if I'm good, I know I'm good. I know best about myself, so a critic doesn't anger me."

— Frank Sinatra

"Nothing anybody's said or written about me ever bothers me, except when it does."

— Frank Sinatra

"Most of my troubles with the press were my own fault. I'll always be grateful to the press for the millions of lines they chose to write which made my name a household word."

— Frank Sinatra

"Frank's audience doesn't care if a girl singer, a comic or an organ grinder with a monkey opens the show. They are there to see him."

— Nancy Sinatra

"You've got to be on the ball from the minute you step out into that spotlight. You gotta know exactly what you're doing every second on that stage, otherwise the act goes right into the bathroom. It's all over. Good night."

— Frank Sinatra

"What formula? I never had one, so I couldn't say what the main ingredient is. I think everybody who's successful in this business has one common ingredient – the talent God gave us. The rest depends upon how it's used."

— Frank Sinatra

"People often remark that I'm pretty lucky. Luck is only important in so far as getting the chance to sell yourself at the right moment. After that, you've got to have talent and know how to use it."

— Frank Sinatra

"It's Frank's world, we're all just livin' in it."

— Dean Martin

"Frank is the only person I know who invited you to a black tie party and, as he is hanging up the telephone says, be sure to bring your sunglasses."

— Harry Kurnitz

"I'm supposed to have a Ph.D. on the subject of women. But the truth is I've flunked more often than not. I'm very fond of women; I admire them. But, like all men, I don't understand them."

— Frank Sinatra

"I love all those girls the same as they love
me. I get thousands of letters a week from
girls who love me. Every time I sing a song,
I make love to them. I'm a boudoir singer."

— Frank Sinatra

"Sinatra's records were on the radio during more deflowerments than those of any other singer's."

— William B. Williams

"Sinatra earned the hold he exerted on the women of his generation. Broads swooned as his intricate emotional specificity created a romantic illusion that in the short run could unlock the door to untold pleasure – while he was singing to them, they could be sure he cared."

— Robert Christgau

"I like intelligent women. When you go out, it shouldn't be a staring contest."

— Frank Sinatra

"The first thing I notice about a woman is her hands. How they're kept. Grooming is so important."

— Frank Sinatra

"When I see a woman who's attractive, it's not a sexual thing – at least, not immediately. I just admire the way she walks, for instance, or her carriage in general, and her general appearance."

— Frank Sinatra

"He treats women as if they were made of glass. He's as concerned with their comfort and dignity as a Victorian."

— Barbara Walters

"He's so gentle. It's as though he thinks I'll break, as though I'm a piece of Dresden china and he's gonna hurt me."

— Ava Gardner

"You treat a lady like a dame, and a dame like a lady."

— Frank Sinatra

"He knows how to make you feel like a complete woman."

— Judith Campbell

"When looking for a woman, it always helps to find a woman who is also looking. Make her feel appreciated, make her feel beautiful. If you practice long enough, you'll know when you get it. And, by the way, 'look, but don't touch.' You can't get into trouble window-shopping."

— Frank Sinatra

"I regard Frank as my extra child. You want to take care of him."

— Judy Garland

"He is the Mercedes-Benz of men."

— Marlene Dietrich

"He's one of the biggest prudes I've ever met. He's an old fashioned man. I've never heard him use a vulgar word in front of a woman."

— Tony Curtis

"I may sound old-fashioned, but I want to think all women should be treated like I want my wife, daughters, and granddaughters to be treated."

— Frank Sinatra

"If there's one thing I don't tolerate, it's a guy who mistreats women. They are the real bullies in life and what they need is a real working over by a man their own size."

— Frank Sinatra

"Never yawn in front of a lady."

— Frank Sinatra

"For years I've nursed a secret desire to spend the Fourth of July in a double hammock with a swingin' redheaded broad – but I could never find me a double hammock."

— Frank Sinatra

"When Sinatra dies, they're giving his zipper to the Smithsonian."

— Dean Martin

"I don't mind being accused of loving women – just never accuse me of hating one."

— Frank Sinatra

"You can be the most artistically perfect performer in the world, but an audience is like a broad – if you're indifferent, Endsville."

— Frank Sinatra

"If I had as many love affairs as you have given me credit for, I'd now be speaking to you from a jar at the Harvard Medical School."

— Frank Sinatra

"A man doesn't know what happiness is until he's married. By then it's too late."

— Frank Sinatra

"Women – I don't know what the hell to make of them. Maybe all that happens is you get older and you know less."

— Frank Sinatra

"Rock 'n' roll smells phony and false. It is sung, played and written, for the most part, by cretinous goons. And, by means of its almost imbecilic reiteration, and sly, lewd and in plain fact, dirty lyrics. It manages to be the martial music of every side-burned delinquent on the face of the earth. It's the most brutal, ugly, desperate, vicious form of expression it has been my misfortune to hear."

— Frank Sinatra

"Rock 'n' roll people love Frank Sinatra, because Frank Sinatra has got what we want. Swagger and attitude. Bad attitude. Frank's the Chairman of the Bad."

— Bono

(On Ava Gardner) "I love her, and God damn me for it."

— Frank Sinatra

(On Tony Bennett) "He the best singer in the business. He excites me when I watch him. He moves me. He's the singer who gets across what the composer has in mind, and probably a little more."

— Frank Sinatra

(On Marlon Brando) "He is the most overrated actor in the world."

— Frank Sinatra

(On Don Rickles) "I like him. But that's because I have no taste.'"

— Frank Sinatra

(On teetotaler Joey Bishop) "He has the distinction of being the only man alive who has ever eaten a dry olive."

— Frank Sinatra

(On Mabel Mercer) "She taught me everything I know."

— Frank Sinatra

(On Peggy Lee) "Her wonderful talent should be studied by all vocalists; her regal presence is pure elegance and charm."

— Frank Sinatra

(On Tommy Dorsey) "He was simpatico about vocalizing, because the instrument he played had the same physical qualities as the human voice."

— Frank Sinatra

(On Nelson Riddle) "He is the greatest arranger in the world, the finest musician with the
biggest bag of tricks."

— Frank Sinatra

"(On Sophia Loren) "She's the mostess!"

— Frank Sinatra

(On John Wayne) "For over half a century he has served honorably as America's symbol to the world of the highest morals and prudent standards of our society."

— Frank Sinatra

(On the resignation of President Richard Nixon) *"Any man can make a mistake."*

— Frank Sinatra

(On Nelson Riddle) "He is the greatest arranger in the world, the finest musician with the
biggest bag of tricks."

— Frank Sinatra

(On Sammy Davis, Jr.) "He goes to the refrig-
erator for a snack, opens the door, and when
the light hits him, he does 45 minutes of his
act!"

— Frank Sinatra

(On Sammy Davis Jr.'s death) "It was a gener-
ous God who gave him to us for all these
years. Sam was the best friend a man could
have."

— Frank Sinatra

(On Dean Martin's death) "Dean has been like the air I breathe. He was my brother. Not through blood but by choice. Our friendship has traveled down many roads over the years, and there will always be a special place in my heart and soul for Dean."

— Frank Sinatra

(On Jack Daniels) "This is a gentleman's drink."

— Frank Sinatra

(On smoking) "Tell 'em, you die your way,
I'll die mine."

— Frank Sinatra

(On Angie Dickinson) "How wonderful it is to meet a lady who's a gentleman."

— Frank Sinatra

(On Ella Fitzgerald) "She, in my opinion, is
the greatest of all contemporary jazz singers."

— Frank Sinatra

(On Lou Rawls) "He's got the classiest singing and silkiest chops in the singing game."

— Frank Sinatra

(On Ray Charles) "He's the only genius in show business."

— Frank Sinatra

"The greatest change in my life began the night they gave me the Oscar. It's funny about that statue – I don't think any actor can experience something like that and not change."

— Frank Sinatra

"I'm for anything that gets you through the night, be it prayer, tranquilizers, or a bottle of Jack Daniels. But to me religion is a deeply personal thing in which man and God go it alone together, without the witch doctor in the middle."

— Frank Sinatra

"I drink to the confusion of our enemies."

— Frank Sinatra

"He always remembered what you drank. He'd met a person once and know she liked white wine, that he liked Martinis, that some-one else drank Manhattans. I could never get over that."

— Ed McMahon

"Alcohol may be man's worst enemy, but the bible says love your enemy."

— Frank Sinatra

"He made drinking an asset. He made it romantic."

— Jonathan Schwartz

"I'm a snob. I am. Aren't we all, to a certain extent? I mean, I won't tolerate certain things, like being crowded into corners. And not enough ice in my drink."

— Frank Sinatra

"Frank distains water. He might rinse his mouth with it after brushing his teeth, but that would be it. If it wasn't mixed with Jack Daniels, he wasn't too interested."

— Hank Cattaneo

"I may run for the office of President. Gimme a bottle and a glass and I'll get America off its ass."

— Frank Sinatra

"I don't drink that sissy stuff, for Christ's sake! You drink the white wine!"

— Frank Sinatra

"I feel sorry for people who don't drink. When they wake up in the morning, that's as good as they're going to feel all day."

— Frank Sinatra

"I don't trust anybody who doesn't drink.
There's something wrong with him."

— Frank Sinatra

"Milk is bad for you. Ask Pat Boone."

— Frank Sinatra

"Fresh air makes me throw up. I can't handle it. I'd rather be around three Denobili cigars blowing in my face all night."

— Frank Sinatra

"I've learned to appreciate the finer things in life. I work hard. I deserve them."

— Frank Sinatra

"If you possess something but you can't give it away, then you don't possess it – it possesses you."

— Frank Sinatra

"I am a symmetrical man, almost to a fault. I demand everything in its place. My clothing must hang just so."

— Frank Sinatra

"For me, a tuxedo is a way of life."

— Frank Sinatra

"Cock your hat – angles are attitudes."

— Frank Sinatra

"No one wore a hat like Dad did."

— Tina Sinatra

"The hat was his crown, cocked askew, as defiant as he was."

— Bill Zehme, *Esquire Magazine*

"What I do with my life is of my own doing.
I live it the best way I can."

— Frank Sinatra

"He has an insatiable desire to live every moment to its fullest because, I guess, he feels that right around the corner is extinction."

— Brad Dexter

"Stay alive, stay active, and get as much practice as you can."

— Frank Sinatra

"I can't work well except under pressure. If there's too much time available, I don't like it – not enough stimulus."

— Frank Sinatra

"He bores easily. If directors keep him busy, he maintains an easy truce; for having started something, Sinatra's next goal is to finish it – but fast."

— Frank Capra

"What bores me loses me."

— Frank Sinatra

"The big lesson in life, baby, is never be
scared of anyone or anything."

— Frank Sinatra

"When Sinatra walks into a room, tension walks in beside him."

— Stanley Kramer

"There's this thing in Sinatra that sort of demands that you respect what he does, or you'll get your ass kicked."

— Pete Hamill

"The only man in town I'd be afraid to fight is Sinatra. I might knock him down, but he'd keep getting up until one of us was dead."

— Robert Mitchum

"Don't tell me. Suggest. But don't tell me."

— Frank Sinatra

"Don't get even, get mad."

— Frank Sinatra

"The best revenge is massive success."

— Frank Sinatra

"He gets up in the morning, and God throws money at him."

— Don Rickles

"You buy a Ferrari when you want to be some-body. You buy a Lamborghini when you are somebody."

— Frank Sinatra

"Don't hide your scars. They make you who you are."

— Frank Sinatra

"Dare to wear the foolish clown face."

— Frank Sinatra

"Frank is a great wit, a real kook."

— Jilly Rizzo

"He's the kind of guy that when he dies, he's going up to heaven and give God a bad time for making him bald."

— Marlon Brando

"He is calm on the outside – inwardly a million things are happening to him."

— Dick Bakalyan

"Frank is the most fascinating man in the world, but don't stick your hand in the cage."

— Tommy Dorsey

"I'm too much of a volatile man. I admire someone who can walk away after being needled, quietly ignoring the whole thing."

— Frank Sinatra

"I'm not one of those complicated, mixed-up cats. I'm not looking for the secret to life. I just go on from day to day, taking what comes."

— Frank Sinatra

"To him, colors enhance life."

— Tina Sinatra

"Orange is the happiest color."

— Frank Sinatra

"Fear is the enemy of logic. There is no more debilitating, crushing, self-defeating, sickening thing in the world – to an individual or to a nation."

— Frank Sinatra

"I believe in you and me. I'm like Albert Schweitzer and Bertrand Russell and Albert Einstein in that I have a respect for life – in any form. I believe in nature, in the birds, the sea, the sky, in everything I can see or that there is real evidence for. If these things are what you mean by God, then I believe in God. But I don't believe in a personal God to whom I look for comfort or for a natural on the next roll of the dice."

— Frank Sinatra

"There are things about organized religion which I resent. Christ is revered as the Prince of Peace, but more blood has been shed in His name than any other figure in history. You show me one step forward in the name of religion and I'll show you a hundred retro-gressions."

— Frank Sinatra

"I'm for decency. Period. I'm for anything
and everything that bodes love and considera-
tion for my fellow man. But when lip service
to some mysterious deity permits bestiality on
Wednesday and absolution on Sunday – cash
me out."

— Frank Sinatra

"Never accept anything without question. Never ignore an inner voice that tells you something could be better, even when other people tell you it's okay."

— Frank Sinatra

"If you don't know the guy on the other side of the world, love him anyway because he's just like you. He has the same dreams, the same hopes and fears. It's one world, pal. We're all neighbors."

— Frank Sinatra

"Whoever he tipped could go buy a mansion in Paris."

— Don Rickles

"A friend is never an imposition."

— Frank Sinatra

"I actually lived with Frank for a while in the fifties. It was the most wonderful year I've ever spent in my life. At the time I was very depressed because my wife had just passed away, but he was so very kind to me. Frank has this great facility for worrying about people who need him."

— Jule Styne

"If you say to Frank, 'I'm having a problem,'
it becomes his problem."

— Burt Lancaster

"A friend to me has no race, no class and belongs to no minority. My friendships are formed out of affection, mutual respect and a feeling of having something in common. These are eternal values that cannot be classified."

— Frank Sinatra

"He is an extraordinary friend. Once he commits himself to a friendship, Frank is a man you can call in the middle of the night; he is the one person you should turn to in an emergency because he will never fail you."

— Irving Lazar

"To be Frank's friend is like one of his songs, 'All or Nothing at All." It is a total, unconditional commitment, a never-fraying security blanket."

— Rosalind Russell

"If they remain loyal, then there is nothing Sinatra will not do in turn. They are wise to remember, however, one thing. He is Sinatra. The Boss."

— Gay Talese

"Where anything is organized by Sinatra, the arrangements are made with legendary efficiency and generosity."

— David Niven

"Sinatra was known for impulsive, awesome acts of generosity – a kindness that was also an assertion of power."

— Ruth Conte

"Frank was a guy that if he liked you, you were his friend forever, and if he didn't like you, you were his enemy forever."

— Larry King

"I always felt I could call and say, 'Frank, I'm in trouble. I need a hundred thousand dollars.'"

— Jo Stafford

"I went to Frank's house in Palm Springs a few years ago when his parents were there. They were cooking an Italian dinner and he was helping. His parents were beautiful people and Frank was as kind and courteous a host as you could wish to meet. He may be tough with the press who don't treat him right, but in private he is a real gentleman."

— Hoagy Carmichael

"Sinatra seemed the embodiment of the hard-drinking, hedonistic swinger who could have his pick of women and who was the leader of a party-loving entourage."

— Stephen Holden, *The New York Times*

"The success of the Rat Pack or the Clan was due to the camaraderie, the three guys who work together and kid each other and love each other."

— Sammy Davis, Jr.

"Frank has worked long and hard for us, his public, for the last 30 years, with his head, with his voice, but especially with his heart. We are all very fortunate to still have this man, the blue eyes, those wonderful blue eyes, and that smile – the greatest entertainer of the 20th century."

— Rosalind Russell

"Frank Sinatra, who has the phrasing, who has the control, who understands the composers; who knows what losing means, as so many have, who made the great comeback, who stands still – eternally – on top of the entertainment world. Ladies and gentlemen, from here on in, it's Frank Sinatra!"

— Howard Cosell

"Frank Sinatra taught me how to do him. It took me seven years to master him. He would tell me, tap your foot, Rich, and don't forget to grasp your sleeve."

— Rich Little

"There are moments when it's too quiet. Particularly late at night or early in the mornings. That`s when you know there's something lacking in your life. You just know."

— Frank Sinatra

"The older you get the more conservative you get."

— Frank Sinatra

"I'm not one of those complicated, mixed-up cats. I'm not looking for the secret to life. I just go on from day to day, taking what comes."

— Frank Sinatra

"Be true to yourself. And stay away from the dark thoughts."

— Frank Sinatra

"I am what I am, and I'm not asking myself any questions. The time you start talking to yourself is when you're unhappy, when you want to change. I don't want to change. I'm satisfied with what I am."

— Frank Sinatra

"He is a man heavier than the Empire State, more connected than the Twin Towers, as recognizable as the Statue of Liberty."

— Bono

"Those who have talent must hug it, embrace it, nurture it and share it lest it be taken away from you as fast as it was loaned to you."

— Frank Sinatra

"He lived for singing. He didn't want to spend his life in his pajamas and his robe."

— Tom Dreesen

"I think my real ambition in life is to pass on to others what I know. It took me a long, long time to learn what I now know, and I don't what that to die with me. I'd like to pass that on to younger people."

— Frank Sinatra

"He is a school unto himself. Sinatra endures with a peculiarly dangerous energy untrammeled by nostalgia or cheap sentiment. Undoubtedly there are people who attend his concerts in expectation of a jog down memory lane, but from the moment he strides on stage, they know they're in for something deeper."

— Gary Giddins

"I wish that one of these days somebody would learn to do [my art] so it doesn't die where it is."

— Frank Sinatra

"There are several things I think I would have done if I had the chance again. I would have been a little more patient about getting out into the world. I would have seen to it that I had a more formal education. I would have become an accomplished musician."

— Frank Sinatra

"I think that if you do the best you can in your life, you get your just reward."

— Frank Sinatra

"I'm gonna live 'till I die."

— Frank Sinatra

"I'm next. I ain't scared, either. Everybody I ever knew is already over there." (after the deaths of Sammy Davis Jr., Ava Gardner, Jilly Rizzo and Dean Martin)

— Frank Sinatra

"You gotta love living, because dying's a pain in the ass."

— Frank Sinatra

"You only go around once, but if you play your cards right, once is enough."

— Frank Sinatra

"I'm losing." (his last words)

— Frank Sinatra

"The world has now lost one of the most precious commodities. In all memories, from childhood to romance to the mature years, Frank has been with us in all times. He gave so much of himself and much more than people realized. It is a sad day today because Frank touched everyone in the world."

— Ernest Borgnine

"Frank Sinatra was a man of dreams, passion, strength, loyalty, and gentleness. His selflessness, love, and generosity were the only constants in an ever-changing world."

— Tina Sinatra

"He always had both feet on the ground. He never believed, or allowed himself to believe, any of the fame that surrounded him. He never took the adulation seriously. He never lost touch with the reality of life around him and he began to make the distinction as to who he could reach out to, who he could confide in, who he could trust, who he could believe in."

— Frank Sinatra, Jr.

"One of Sinatra's favorite toasts to make with glass in hand was, 'May you live to be 100 and may the last voice you hear be mine.' The master is gone but his voice will live forever."

— Tony Bennett

"It [Sinatra's music] will endure. My grand-children will listen to him 50 years from now."

— Pete Hamill

"He was the greatest entertainer of all time, the voice of several decades. His contribution to music is as significant as Picasso's was to art."

— Robert Davi

"Sinatra held the patent, the original blue-print, on singing the popular song."

— Mel Tormé

"Sinatra was able to turn a 32-bar song into a three-act play ."

— Julius LaRosa

"Sinatra was a pop music legend, not a civic leader or entrepreneur. But Sinatra was a one-man chamber of commerce who gave Las Vegas something equally important: an image."

— Mike Weatherford,
Las Vegas Review-Journal

"Frank Sinatra was the epitome of American male coolness. When he walked into any room, his confident swagger created an electric charge. Women wanted to be with him and men wanted to be him."

— Brett McKay, *The Art of Manliness*

"Sinatra was a stylist. He also had a great instrument and phenomenal range. And he was a terrific actor. It's that component in the performances that I thought was inherently theatrical."

— Twyla Tharp

"Loneliness is the key to understanding Sinatra, both the man, who dreaded solitude yet so often felt alone in the entourages with which he surrounded himself and the audiences before whom he performed, and the musician. Even his songs of joy – and no one could express unbounded happiness more thrillingly in his singing than Sinatra – were manifestations of his fundamental loneliness."

— Michael Nelson

"Controversy, suffering, angst were all part of the Sinatra DNA. Without those tortured feelings, perhaps his songs would not resonate like they do."

— Charlene Giannetti,
Frank Sinatra: The One and Only Voice

"I knew Sinatra the private man very well – a side of him that is in total contrast to his mercurial public image. He is one of the dearest and humanistic people I have ever met."

— Alec Wilder

"Frank Sinatra's voice expresses more eloquence that I can ever say in mere words."

— Billy Joel

"Sinatra enunciated his words with a casual sophistication that defined his notion of class. But underneath there was always Hoboken, in all its immigrant insularity and street swagger. With every phrase, he turned English into American and American into music."

— Robert Christgau

"On behalf of all New Jersey, Frank, I want to say, 'Hail, brother, you sang out our soul.'"

— Bruce Springsteen

"He was the epitome of what singing is all about, beautiful sounds, smooth as silk, effortless, impeccable phrasing, stylish, intelligent and full of heart."

— Barbara Streisand

"Sinatra transformed popular singing by infusing lyrics with a personal, intimate point of view that conveyed a steady current of eroticism."

— Stephen Holden

"We have lost part of our capacity to self-reflect because Frank is gone. His music helped us understand our own lives more clearly because he was authentically honest about himself. I am so sad for all of us who are now without him."

— Shirley MacLaine

"Frank knew how to do it. Everything. It humbles me to have been a small part of his gigantic presence."

— Quincy Jones

"He was the first love of my life and he remained a true friend, always there when I needed him. I will miss him more than words can say."

— Mia Farrow

"He brought unmatched excitement to the Strip and defined the word 'swinger' for all times. With his little gang of merry men he established forever a sense of free-floating fun and frolic that captured the imagination of the world."

— Gregory Peck

"Sinatra was what a nightclub was all about. He brought everything you wanted to a nightclub: the mystery, the excitement….. the ring-a-ding guy."

— Alan King

"There was something about the man larger than the man himself."

— Barbara Rush

"Sinatra transformed popular singing by infusing lyrics with a personal, intimate point of view that conveyed a steady current of eroticism. Almost singlehandedly, he helped lead a revival of vocalized swing music that took American pop to a new level of musical sophistication. He was a singularly incandescent vocal phenomenon."

— Stephen Holden, *The New York Times*

"Frank Sinatra was a talented and tempera-
mental balladeer who dominated popular
music longer than any entertainer before him
and clung to his legendary life as tenaciously
as he had stuck with the audiences he loved.
His masterful interpretation and flawless
execution of some of America's most beloved
songs earned his reputation as the most influ-
ential popular singer of the 20th century."

— Burt A. Folkart, *The Los Angeles Times*

"There will never be another Frank Sinatra. He is all by himself with what he's done with his life as a performer and as a man."

— Vic Damone

SELECTED BIBLIOGRAPHY

Zehme, Bill, *The Way You Wear Your Hat: Frank Sinatra and the Lost Art of Livin'* (Harper Collins, 1997)

Summers, Anthony, *Sinatra: The Life* (Vintage, 2007)

O'Brien, E. and Wilson, Robert, *Sinatra 101: Best Recordings and the Stories Behind Them* (Berkley Trade, 1996)

Hamill, Pete, *Why Sinatra Matters* (Back Bay Books, 2003)

Mustazza, Leonard, *Ol' Blue Eyes: A Frank Sinatra Encyclopedia* (Praeger, 1999)

Petkov, Steven and Mustazza, Leonard, *The Frank Sinatra Reader* (Oxford University Press, 1995)

Talese, Gay, *Frank Sinatra Has a Cold and Other Essays* (Penguin Books, 2011)

Rockwell, John, *Sinatra: An American Classic* (Random House, 1984)

Lahr, John, *Sinatra: The Artist and the Man* (Random House, 1997)

Turner, John Frayn, *Frank Sinatra* (Taylor Trade Publishing, 2004)

Freedland, Michael, *All the Way: A Biography of Frank Sinatra* (St. Martin's Press, 1997)

Havers, Richaer, *Sinatra* (Dorling Kindersley Verlag, 2005)

Mustazza, Leonard and Granata, Charles L., *Frank Sinatra and Popular Culture: Essays on an American Icon* (Praeger, 1998)

Douglas-Home, Robin, *Sinatra* (Grossett & Dunlap, 1962)

Vare, Ethlie Ann, *Legend: Frank Sinatra and the American Dream* (Boulevard, 1995)

Coleman, Ray, *Sinatra: Portrait of the Artist* (Regnery Publishing, 1998)

Hanna, David, *Sinatra: Ol' Blue Eyes Remembered* (Bell, 1998)

Stolley, Richard B., *Sinatra: An Intimate Portrait of a Very Good Year* (Stewart, Tabori and Chang, 2002)

Shaw, Arnold, *Sinatra: Twentieth-Century Romantic* (Holt, Rinehart and Winston, 1968)

Clarke, Donald, *All or Nothing at All: A Life of Frank Sinatra* (Fromm International, 1997)

Kaplan, James, *Frank: The Voice* (Anchor, 2011)

42567556R00128

Made in the USA
Lexington, KY
28 June 2015